Heart To Soul

From my heart to your soul

Akshika Mittal

Dedication

"To my parents, whose unwavering love and support have shaped me into who I am; to my grandparents, whose wisdom and kindness continue to inspire me; to my aunt, for her constant encouragement and belief in me; and to my friends, for their laughter, loyalty, and understanding. This book is also for every pure soul out there, whose light makes the world a better place."

Preface

This book is the result of years of reflection, learning, and growth. It has been a journey filled with moments of doubt, discovery, and inspiration, and I am deeply grateful for the support of those who have been by my side through it all.
This book is also dedicated to every pure soul out there, whose kindness and light make the world a better place.
May the words within these pages resonate with you, just as your presence has impacted my life in ways I will forever cherish.

Acknowledgements

Writing this book has been a deeply personal journey, and I could not have completed it without the support of so many incredible people.

First, I want to express my deepest gratitude to my parents. Your love, guidance, and sacrifices have shaped every part of me. Thank you for always believing in me, even when I doubted myself. To my grandparents, your wisdom and kindness have been a constant source of inspiration throughout my life.

To my aunt, whose faith in me never wavered—thank you for your constant encouragement and for always being there with open arms and an open heart.

To my friends, who have filled my life with joy, laughter, and support. Your belief in me has kept me going through the toughest of times.

Lastly, to every pure soul out there—your kindness, light, and resilience inspire me every day. This book is as much yours as it is mine.

Thank you to everyone who has been a part of this journey. Each of you has left an indelible mark on my heart.

Take a bullet for you

You don't know the way I feel for you,
I could take a bullet for you yeah

You are my daily dose of sunshine,
That piece of my heart nobody can find

You are like heat waves in the chills of winter,
A slice of cake when mouth tastes bitter

You don't know the way I feel for you,
I could take a bullet for you yeah

You are like a bucket of my happiness,
The ocean full of utter brightness

You are the way to my paradise,
The desire of my whole life

You don't know the way I feel for you,
I could take a bullet for you yeah

Take a bullet for you yeah
Take a bullet for you..

I need you

The conversations I had with you
Is now the only thing I'm left to
The memories I made with you
Is now the only thing I've left to hold on to

I wanna kiss you
I wanna hug you
I wanna say I love you

Even though you don't deserve my love
And I know that you're not right for me
But I still want you
Oh baby I need you
Yeah

Your name engraved on my heart
Your picture embedded on my brain
Your memory flowing through my veins
Your voice echoing in my ears

I wanna feel you
I wanna hold you
I wanna say I miss you

Even though you don't deserve my love
And I know that you're not right for me
But I still want you
Oh baby I need you
Yeah

I wanted to be the reason of your smile
But you became the reason of my pain
You were like the flame to my candle
But you ended it's warmth by blowing it away

I wanna see you
I wanna touch you
I wanna say I care for you

Even though you don't deserve my love
And I know that you're not right for me
But I still want you
Oh baby I need you
Yeah

Believe me girl

You're the sweetest girl I've ever met
Believe me girl

I just wanna make you mine
I just wanna see you smile
I love the way you shine
It always blows my mind

You're the most beautiful girl I've ever met
Believe me girl

I'm so mesmerized by you
I feel complete with you
Oh girl, you make me better everytime I see you

You're the most magical girl I've ever met
Believe me girl

I promise I'll love you till my last breath
And I'll keep you closest to my heart

No nobody can take you away from me
Oh girl, now you are the most important part of my life

You're the sweetest girl I've ever met
Believe me girl

Heavy

It's getting heavier day by day
The love I have for each one of you

It's getting heavier day by day
The trust I have on each one of you

It's getting heavier day by day
The feelings I keep holding on to

It's getting heavier day by day
The thoughts I'm going through

I keep asking myself
Why go through this burden though?

Do they deserve this?
Why be carrying this burden though?

It's getting heavier day by day
The love I have for each one of you

My body, mind, heart and soul
Pressurizing me to let it go

The want to in my eyes
The desire to stay alive

But it's getting heavier day by day
And I know that it will always stay

Shape of a diamond

You broke me and my heart
Into a million pieces
So I collected them and assembled them Into the shape of
a diamond
Yeah shape of a diamond

Now it has sharp edges
So no one can enter it
And mess with me
Like the way you did to me
Now it shines bright
And reflect back
All the negativity around me

You broke my heart into a million pieces
So I assembled them into
The shape of a diamond

Now it has glass walls
So you can look at yourself

before you do something to me
Now it takes heat
so I absorb the warmth
I get from my loved ones easily

You broke my heart into a million pieces
So I assembled them into
The shape of a diamond

Now it's both dangerous and beautiful
Can make you both bleed or gorgeous
And that truly depends on your behaviour

You broke my heart into a million pieces
So I assembled them into
The shape of a diamond
Yeah shape of a diamond

The old one

I ain't nobody's priority
So I make myself my priority

No I don't beg for relations anymore
I connect with myself more everyday

If you mess with me, I'll cut you off my life
I ain't the old one anymore

You think you know me baby
But I am more than your mind can intake

Ya I don't need none of your pity
I have my own ways cause I'm gritty

If you mess with me, I'll cut you off my life
I ain't the old one anymore

The more I love, the more I got hurt
The more I trust, the more I got deceived

This made me stopped doing both
Which made me turn into a rock

Heartless, but strong
Emotionless, but brave

If you mess with me, I'll cut you off my life
I ain't the old one anymore

I don't know

I'm not like others or probably the vice versa.
I don't know.

I am feeling too much or the world is heartless.
I don't know.

I am positive or the world supports negativity.
I don't know.

I relate too much or the world is not worthy.
I don't know.

I am falling or it's it's depth.
I don't know.

I am strong or am I the weakest.
I don't know.

So easily?

It's time for me to let him go..
But how do I extract someone from my heart so easily?

He left, but his memories stayed with me in my head..
How do I let go those memories so easily?

He took away a part of my soul, and he didn't even
know..
How do I forget about that part of my soul so easily?

He didn't even love me..
But where do I throw the love I have for him so easily?

I loved him so much that it hurted me like hell..
How do I heal that hurt so easily?

He took away my happiness with him..
How do I hide my tears behind my smile so easily?

Worthless

You know what I hate about myself?
Loving you, missing you and dying for you

Made my life worthless
Just coz you were shrewd

Lost my mind, heart and soul
Just to offend your actions of discourteous

Started off on a beautiful note
Turned out to be the biggest mistake of my life

Oh what I have done to myself?

Deep down I know you don't deserve my love
Still I crave for your presence

How do I jump out of this well?
Where I can see a dark end

Look what you've done to me
Loving you is now a compulsion for me

People say time will take you away from my heart
But I know you'll always be there like a hole in my heart

Why did god send you to my life?
Just for you to play with me like that?

Your eyes

Your eyes
They can never tell lies
I can see right through them

Your eyes
They can't handle goodbyes
I can see right through them

Your eyes
They glow when you see me
I can see right through them

Your eyes
They whisper love to me
I can see right through them

Your eyes
They are like diamonds
I can see right through them

Felt it right

It was when I felt it right
The scorching sun was heated tight

It was when I felt it right
You were walking to me upright

It was when I felt it right
The battle of your face to hair is delight

It was when I felt it right
Your playful eyes make me excite

It was when I felt it right
The curves of your body gave me insight

It was when I felt it right
The moon shines bright

Embrace

Let the warmth of our embrace
Make you forget all your pains

Let the warmth of our embrace
Make your sorrows misplace

Let the warmth of our embrace
Relieve you from your anxiousness

Let the warmth of our embrace
Assure you that I'm gonna stay

Let the warmth of our embrace
Set you free from all your fears

Let the warmth of our embrace
Allow me to love you forever

Universe

The universe showers blessings
Supporting in our endless battles
Building our faith in them

You can find them through utter peace
Within self or outer breeze

When I was falling in too deep
A nightmare of a dark tunnel
I could feel your hand for help
Through which I pulled out myself

The universe showers blessings
To keep you stand upright
And held your head high

You can find them through utter peace
Within self or outer breeze

Just the two of us

Holding hands, your head on my shoulder
Lets keep it for just the two of us

Endless cuddles, your feet on my feet
Lets keep it for just the two of us

Walking together, your fingers in my fist
Lets keep it for just the two of us

Kissing your forehead, your soul in my body
Lets keep it for just the two of us

Surrendering into each other's arms
Lets keep it for just the two of us

More "you"

Could you be more "you"
The shelter when I need to hide from the world

Could you be more "you"
The support when I need to fight from the world

Could you be more "you"
The survival I need to breathe in this world

Could you be more "you"
The calmness when I get anxious in this world

Could you be more "you"
To live my life with you in this world

Ecstasy

When you touch me gently
Your love is a form of ecstasy

When you care for me emotionally
Your love is a form of ecstasy

When you make me laugh through rough times
Your love is a form of ecstasy

When we dance around slowly
Your love is a form of ecstasy

When you open your arms for me
Your love is a form of ecstasy

Power of faith

The power of faith
Takes you on the peak

The power of faith
Takes you to the supreme

The power of faith
Takes you on the righteous path

The power of faith
Takes you through the bizarre

The power of faith
Makes you cross the pain

The power of faith
Makes you achieve your desires

The power of faith
Takes you to the serenity of the soul

Butterfly wings

Take a leap and go for it
I'll be your butterfly wings

Take my hand and move forward
I'll be your butterfly wings

Step by step you will conquer the world
I'll be your butterfly wings

You'll get through all your sufferings
I'll be your butterfly wings

I will never leave you my love as
I'm your butterfly wings

A letter to my baby sisters

Many people would call you beautiful, some would see
you as a princess, as a doll or as an angel. I know you are
and always be all of the above.
But I wish a whole lot of STRENGTH in your mind, heart
and soul for your life.
I can't tell you that I'll always be there with you, but I'll
promise to always love you, and try to be your best
sister.

A letter to my best friend

To my best buddy

You are my safest place
Where I can share my everything

You're like my punching bag
That also hits me back, lol

I love being silly with you
And laughing out till our stomach hurts

Hanging out with you is the best part of my day
And I don't know why you remind me of the song "stay"
Cause I'll be fucked up if you can't be right here, ooo,
ooooo

We go through ups and downs, we share our joys and
sorrows with each other
I just wanna let you know that I'll always be there for
you no matter what

The way you protect me, by saving me from the ball or
by saving me from the dog
I'll always protect you from getting hurt or when you're
falling apart

I may not be your bestest friend but you'll always be my
forever best friend
I love you and I'll definitely miss you when we part our
ways..

Dear mom

Dear mom,

When I hug you,
I revive myself for being me.

When I see you're smile,
I know it's gonna be fine.

When I see you're tears,
I find my heart as a hollow part.

When I look up at you,
I believe there's always a way out.

When I see you,
I can't imagine my life without you!

www.ingramcontent.com/pod-product-compliance
Lightning Source LLC
La Vergne TN
LVHW010022200726
843495LV00015B/1887